THE KEY
To Revival
FORGIVENESS

By Dr. Alan Pateman

BY DR. JENNIFER PATEMAN

AVAILABLE FROM APMI PUBLICATIONS, AMAZON.COM AND OTHER RETAIL OUTLETS

THE KEY

To Revival

FORGIVENESS

DR. ALAN PATEMAN

BOOK TITLE:
Forgiveness, the Key to Revival

WRITTEN BY Dr. ALAN PATEMAN
ISBN: 978-1-909132-41-2
eBook ISBN: 978-1-909132-42-9

Published By:
APMI Publications
In Partnership with Truth for the Journey Books **12**
Email: publications@alanpateman.com
www.AlanPatemanMinistries.com

Acknowledgements:
Author/Design/Senior Editor/Publisher: Apostle Dr. Alan Pateman
Editing/Proofreading/Research: Dr. Jennifer Pateman
Computer Administration/Office Manager: Dr. Dorothea Struhlik
Cover Image Credit: www.PosterMyWall.com

Unless otherwise indicated, Scripture quotations are taken from the Amplified® Bible, Copyright © 1954, 1958, 1962, 1964, 1965, 1987 by The Lockman Foundation. Used by permission. (www.Lockman.org)

*Where scriptures appear with special emphasis (**in bold**, italic or <u>underlined</u>) we have edited them ourselves in order to bring focused attention within the context of this subject being taught.*

❖

Dedication

To my wife Jenny and our
three children, Andrew James,
Naomi and Abigail.

❖

Acknowledgements

I want to thank all of my friends and colleagues who have endorsed this book by contributing to its publication. Your selfless support is truly admirable. I appreciate each and everyone of you, your families, ministries and churches.

Apostle Dr. Benjamin Ayim Asare
Followers of Christ Int. Church
Novara, Italy
bayimasare@yahoo.it
www.benjaminayimasareministries.com

Pastors Dr. Tony & Josie Botfield
Oasis Christian Fellowship Telford
Telford, United Kingdom
ukdirector@alanpateman.com
www.oasischristianfellowshiptelford.com

Apostle George Hooper
Lifegate Christian Ministries Intl.
Verona, Italy
georper@inwind.it
www.lifegatechristianchapel.org

Rev. Blessing Ogbonmwan
European Coordinator:
Christ Apostolic Church of God Mission
Merksem, Antwerp, Belgium
cacgmbelgiumparish@yahoo.com
www.cacgmfaithworkscenter.org

Alan Jr and Rebecca Pateman
Kingdom Expanse
Bückeburg, Germany
media@kingdomexpanse.com
www.kingdomexpanse.com

Pastor David Quarshie
Christian Praise Int. Centre
Boves, Italy
davidquarshie2007@yahoo.it

❖

Table of Contents

❖

Introduction

Within this small but powerful book I want to speak and focus on the all-important subject of forgiveness *(including repentance)*. My trigger for this was something that I came across via the Internet, a joint interview *(back in January 2013)* between Todd Bentley and the Founders of the God Channel, Rory and Wendy Alec.

It was totally unpredictable that I would be moved by such an interview, because I had previously been quite indifferent. However to my surprise it stirred something in me, regardless of any prior misgivings about the Lakeland revival and its controversy.

I learnt early on in my life and ministry that controversy was the rule rather than the exception. I accepted this once I realised that Jesus' ministry was never free of controversy - then or now. The loss of reputation is not rare to the ministry nor is being misunderstood or misrepresented, it comes with the territory.

❖

CHAPTER 1

Forgiveness
Precedes your Next Level

All of us should be interested in what God is doing in the earth today, how He is doing it and who He is doing it through. On a personal level, I am willing to lay down any preconceived notions about anything, especially if I can see God moving. Regardless of what has gone before.

I refuse to be trapped by my comfort zone, which keeps me from seeing or hearing God. If any believer/leader is more loyal to his comfort zone, than to God, he/she will always feel on the outside looking in.

However there is a spiritual law that cannot be revoked anymore than gravity and that is the law of forgiveness. Scripture is absolute when it comes to forgiveness. IF we forgive, THEN we are forgiven. It's that simple but no one said it was easy! Nonetheless, forgiveness can be likened to a spiritual key that unlocks spiritual doors and opportunities! **"He who opens and no one shuts, and shuts and no one opens"** *(Revelation 3:7 NKJV)*. Or as one other translation puts it: "The One who possesses the key of David, which **opens the possibilities** so that no one can shut them. The One who **closes all options** so that no one can open" *(VOICE)*.

When we forgive, a RELEASE takes place that can catapult us into our future and our destiny. But vice versa is also true. All of us remain in bondage when we refuse to forgive. We self injure and self-destruct when we choose not to forgive.

After Lakeland, most folks could not hear of Todd Bentley anymore, his marriage, tattoos or anything else for that matter because they felt let down or betrayed! Putting such things aside, **I found myself being moved by the Spirit after seeing Todd, Rory and Wendy openly discuss, repent and forgive one another before the entire Body of Christ during that interview.**

The "conviction" that I was left with was that God was definitely in that interview and was doing something new with them all, including the God TV family. I sensed a new day had come to the Body of Christ **FORGIVENESS ALWAYS PRECEDES YOUR NEXT LEVEL.**

It is also true to say, unless you release others you won't be released. "Do not judge, and you will not be judged. Do not condemn, and you will not be condemned. Forgive, and you will be forgiven" *(Luke 6:37 NIV)*.

Such repentance will affect a lot of people globally and usher in a new revival. Today Todd Bentley is being used in revival once again, this time in Pretoria South Africa and God is certainly moving, plus Todd has added maturity and wisdom these days.

In the same way we too can experience a personal revival in all that God has promised for us, as words that have brought curses are broken. We must never underestimate the significance of forgiveness. There is a release of power when forgiveness takes place, both corporately and individually.

On the other hand precious people all over the world, remain in bondage today, because of the words of their own mouths, spoken negatively over themselves or others. The truth is they will never experience personal revival, all the while they are not willing to forgive.

In his book **"The Secret Kingdom"** *(p114)* Pat Robertson wrote about the Law of Reciprocity.

One simple declaration by Jesus revealed a law that will change the world: **"Give, and it will be given to you." Eight words, they form a spiritual principle that touches every relationships, every condition of man, whether spiritual or physical.** They are pivotal in any hope we have... Jesus expanded the universality of this theme throughout His ministry, varying subject matter and application. His point was so encompassing that it demanded many illustrations. In the discourse from which we get the eight words, we find this expansion: "just as you want people to treat you, treat them in the same way." And from that, of course, came what the world describes as the **GOLDEN RULE: "Do unto others as you would have them do unto you."**

Jesus went on, putting a frame around the eight key words in this manner:

Be merciful, just as your Father is merciful. And do not pass judgement and you shall not be judged: and you will be pardoned. Give, and it will be given to you; good measure, pressed down, shaken together, running over, they will pour into your lap, For whatever measure you deal out to others, it will be dealt to you in return.

By putting this together with the world's greatest teaching on love, repeated from the Old Testament by Jesus as the heart of God's will, we establish the perfect "law" for conduct: **"YOU SHALL LOVE YOUR NEIGHBOR AS YOURSELF"** *(Pat Robertson).*

❖

CHAPTER 2

The Anointing flows Down not Up

I t was in 2008 that the Lakeland revival collapsed and a genuine RESTORATION process began. Five years later a public show of humility between Todd Bentley, Rory and Wendy openly discuss, repent and forgive one another before the entire Body of Christ, that interview was a good example to set before the Body.

Leaders are obligated to lead by example and from personal experience I can verify just how effective such a time of open repentance and forgiveness can help to lift spiritual blockades that develop over time - due to sin, division, hurts, burn-out, wrong heart motives and more.

God can't move anywhere, if there is sin in the camp *(where there is no repentance)* or unforgiveness at the helm.

"Precious OIL POURED ON THE HEAD RUNNING DOWN on the beard, RUNNING DOWN on Aaron's beard, DOWN on the collar of his robe" *(Psalm 133:2 NIV)*.

NOTICE HOW THE ANOINTING RUNS "DOWN" NOT UP! The same is true for the Church. The anointing is first poured on the HEAD. This denotes Christ, but also leadership, then to the rest of the Body. So if the leadership does not have their acts together, so that the anointing can flow, this will cut off the flow for the rest of the Body, *(I am talking about the corporate anointing)*.

In vice versa if those in leadership are right with God, then everyone else benefits from the anointing that flows down. It can never be the people's fault that the anointing is not flowing as it should. The responsibility rests with leadership. NEEDLESS TO SAY, WHEN LEADERS ARE RESTORED, IT'S IN THE BEST INTEREST OF EVERYONE! **WE MUST NEVER RESIST RESTORATION.**

Following this interview *(January 2013)* anyhow, I found myself for the rest of that day *(with the leading of the Holy Spirit)* pouring over hours of research. Going through old and new footage, listening to more interviews and much more; praying, thinking and contemplating my previous stance, and seeking God.

I concluded with a renewed sense of humility towards all that the Holy Spirit is doing in the earth today, particularly through the prophetic and apostolic moves. I am fully convinced that such a mood of repentance and forgiveness is necessary for revival, and relevant right now for the entire Body of Christ.

So much RESTORATION is needed, in so many different quarters, right across the board. We simply won't get by without it, corporately or individually. And for such leaders to openly repent, globally, not only in front of select viewers but the entire Body of Christ, was a very healthy new beginning and makes way for the Latter Rain.

In other words, THE BEST IS YET TO COME! And this is not limited to what the God Channel or Todd Bentley is doing, but all about what God is doing. It just so happens that God is using them to reach millions of souls for Christ and this end time harvest needs its labourers. The destroyer comes, but God rebukes the devourer and restoration takes place. Only the Body must not turn against the head *(leadership)* and refuse restoration. This would be detrimental.

The adversary capitalizes on our ignorance, which is why so many of GOD'S PEOPLE perish for the lack of knowledge. *"MY PEOPLE are DESTROYED for lack of knowledge"* (Hosea 4:6 KJV). What is the knowledge they lack? It is the knowledge of God Himself! *(His person, His agenda – what He is doing in the earth and how He is doing it).*

> **<u>MY</u> PEOPLE ARE BEING <u>DESTROYED</u> BECAUSE THEY <u>DON'T KNOW ME</u>.** *SINCE YOU PRIESTS* **REFUSE TO KNOW <u>ME</u>,** *I refuse to recognize you as my priests. Since you have forgotten the laws of your God, I will forget to bless your children.*
>
> *(Hosea 4:6 NLT)*

❖

CHAPTER 3

Finding Stillness
in the Midst of Madness!

In the previous chapter we spoke about God's people perishing for the lack of knowledge about Him. Knowing God is essential. God desires that none should perish. The following scripture reveals that being "still" is part of KNOWING Him.

> *BE STILL, AND KNOW THAT I AM GOD: I will be exalted among the heathen, I will be exalted in the earth. The Lord of hosts is with us; the God of Jacob is our refuge. Selah.*
>
> *(Psalm 46:10-11 KJV)*

"BE STILL AND KNOW - THAT I AM GOD..." We must have clear, intimate knowledge of God. Who He is, what He does, *(and perhaps most importantly)*, what He will never do! We must KNOW HIM PERSONALLY.

However we must recognise the undeniable prerequisite for such intimate knowledge: **"BE STILL!"** The question is: "How?" because stillness is perhaps one of the hardest things for us to achieve in this hyper-driven-technological-age.

The word used for "know" in the Hebrew language means: *"to know (properly, to ascertain by seeing);* used in a great variety of senses including: *discern, discover, feel… and familiar friend"* (Strong's h3045).

Such meanings in the Hebrew would confirm this idea that we must have a **personal-knowledge-of-God.**

Further in the Hebrew language, being "STILL" means: *"to slacken… abate, cease… to let alone, sink,* **DROP AND RELAX.** *To withdraw, refrain, to let go, to be quiet"* (Strong's h7503).

"Letting go" on the inside or even learning to "relax" internally is increasingly difficult for individuals to achieve. At the moment of this writing, there is a current song in the secular charts called, "My Head is a Jungle" *(by Wankelmut & Emma Louise).* Its melody is very hypnotic and its lyrics go *(in part)* like this: *"I'm complicated, you don't get me, I have trouble understanding myself… my head is a jungle."*

I checked the lyrics online and would like to suggest that such a song probably sums up what a vast majority of people identify with. A "jungle" is an apt description of an undisciplined mind.

Some of the most intelligent, talented and creative individuals that this world has ever known have also been recognised as *"complicated and misunderstood!"*

No one seemingly escapes the madness, no matter how brilliant they are. In fact the more brilliant a person is, the more tormented they can be!

In addition, the Young's Literal Translation says: **"DESIST, AND KNOW THAT I [AM] GOD."** It does not use the word "still." However the English word "DESIST" chiefly means: *"to cease, and to stop!"*

How do we be still? Simply "STOP" long enough *(in our busy lives)*, to get to know God. Stop fighting His will and surrender.

This is a word of warning to all of us. People who are always in a hurry; always busy, will find it very hard to hear the voice of God for their lives. They will always have to hear His Voice "through" someone else.

Therefore if we want to know God better, it's imperative that we learn this inward "STILLNESS" – which is a personal discipline that only the Holy Spirit can teach us:

> *[HE HAS GIVEN US A SPIRIT] OF POWER AND OF LOVE AND OF CALM AND WELL-BALANCED MIND AND DISCIPLINE AND SELF-CONTROL.*
> *(2 Timothy 1:7)*

The lost art of stillness! Everything in our day and age is designed to crowd-God-out-of-our-lives. I would suggest also that learning how to be inwardly "STILL" has become a lost-art. Perhaps except for those attempting the counterfeit through yoga or other eastern religions *(via various meditation technics, such as mantras to aid the calming of their minds)*. Everyone is seeking some sanity in the madness! In one temporal form or another - using drugs to force the mood.

Stillness before God however, involves much more than just trendy philosophies and technics. It requires an absolute surrender of the mind towards Him and His Word. Yielding without reserve and in such position there is zero "conflict" just "compliance."

Such meditation can occur inwardly day and night – no matter where we are *(Joshua 1:8)*. It is continual. It is called "relationship." It is "letting go." It is "relaxed." It is "calm!"

> *After the earthquake a fire, but the Lord was not in the fire; and after the fire* **[A SOUND OF GENTLE STILLNESS AND] A STILL, SMALL VOICE.**
>
> *(1 Kings 19:12)*

> *He who is able to hear, let him* **LISTEN TO AND HEED WHAT THE [HOLY] SPIRIT SAYS** *to the assemblies (churches).*
>
> *(Revelation 2:29)*

If we don't recognise His stillness, we will never be able to recognise His voice. Sometimes we are guilty of being tangled up in the affairs of this life, *(with all of its demands)* that we fail to recognise God's voice when He does speak to us.

Another scripture that refers to being "still" is found in the Psalms:

*Stand in awe, [be angry] and sin not: commune with your own heart upon your bed, and **BE STILL**. Selah.*
                                        (Psalm 4:4 KJV [AMP])

*Think long; think hard. When you are angry, don't let it carry you into sin. When night comes, **IN CALM** BE SILENT.*
                                        (Psalm 4:4 VOICE)

The definition of "stillness" exceeds quietness. It means much more than that. It involves being: "*undisturbed by wind, sound or current... calm and deep silence...*" Such a word is vital to our knowledge of God. In His presence is the fullness of joy, but also it's a "stilling" experience. It's the only place we can truly off-load "the cares of this life" and all that *overwhelms*.

In life, there are always those people who manage to take everything in their stride! The more mature a person is, the more they have learnt the art of "stillness." A walk we must all master, which allows the peace of God to act as "umpire" of our hearts and minds [our inner lives] in all situations and circumstances *(Colossians 3:15)*.

*Let the peace (**soul harmony** which comes) from Christ rule (**ACT AS UMPIRE CONTINUALLY**) in your hearts [deciding and settling with finality all questions that arise in your minds, in that peaceful state] to which* *as [members of Christ's] one body you were also called [to live]. And be thankful (appreciative), [giving praise to God always].*

(Colossians 3:15)

So what does a chapter on stillness have to do with forgiveness? Much. Because far too many times we allow the emotions of others, or just the presence of others to stir us up into a frenzy inwardly. Learning stillness is an act of the will, as much as love is *(by loving the unlovable).*

To remain still inwardly, when certain individuals are around, who know how to wind us up. Those we must walk in forgiveness towards, daily. Those who have hurt us, and the very memory of them invoke anger.

Forgiveness is not a feeling. It's an act of obedience that liberates us. The feelings eventually follow. The stillness remains and the anger eventually abates. The storm subsides and calm lasts. Hallelujah!

❖

CHAPTER 4

Restoration
Releases New Hope

art of knowing God, is recognising Him in
action, including what He is doing in the earth
today. One thing we must recognise is God's
work is RESTORATION.

Referring back to the interview with Todd Bentley on
the God Channel, *(as mentioned in a previous chapter)*, I did
and have developed a renewed respect for Rory and Wendy
Alec. At which point I was not interested in hearing all the
opinions of others, but just God's WILL on the subject! HIS
WILL IS <u>ALWAYS</u> ONE OF "RESTORATION."

We must never lose sight of the fact that the working of
the Holy Spirit includes the ministry of RECONCILIATION
AND RESTORATION. In fact in many ways this is the

FORGIVENESS, THE KEY TO REVIVAL

lifeblood of the Body of Christ, without it, we cannot corporately move forwards in any real or sustainable way, regardless of what has gone-on before - we are all the wiser for it!

When Benny Hinn reunited with his ex-wife, lots of "debate and chatter" flies around such events. Whether approval or disapproval, judgmental or critical – and it spreads right across the global internet like a contagious-virus!

Even still, I am utterly convinced that people still want to see the power of restoration in demonstration, despite their doubts. It gives them hope in their own situations. Most people would be willing for the time it takes for restoration to be fully effected, so long as restoration takes place and restoration takes TIME. But during such TIME God can do many mighty things!

I have learnt and re-learnt in my own life, that when nothing seems to be happening, often that's when most is happening! Like Hosea 4 tells us, we must KNOW our God. We must know how God the Holy Spirit is on the job 24/7 and technically there is never a time when God is not working, moving, hovering, brooding, fixing, healing, answering... but it is only as we trust Him that RESTORATION can take place and His perfect will fulfilled in our lives, *(see Psalm 125:1; Isaiah 40:31; Jeremiah 17:7-8; Proverbs 28:25).*

The only people who qualify for all the promises found in the bible are those who actively TRUST God everyday of their lives. WE ONLY QUALIFY IF WE HAVE A LIVING **TRUST** IN GOD.

*I WILL SAY OF THE LORD, HE IS MY REFUGE AND MY FORTRESS, MY GOD; ON HIM I LEAN AND RELY, AND **IN HIM I [CONFIDENTLY] TRUST!***

(Psalm 91:2)

*MY REFUGE, AND MY BULWARK, **MY GOD, I TRUST IN HIM.***

(Psalm 91:2 YLT)

The message of restoration is all powerful because it totally rebuffs hopelessness, which is very important since hopelessness can cause heart-sickness; *"Hope deferred makes the heart sick" (Proverbs 13:12 KJV).* RESTORATION SENDS OUT THE UNMISTAKABLE MESSAGE THAT GOD IS BIGGER THAN ALL THE CIRCUMSTANCES, THE OPINIONS OF MEN, EVERY SPIRITUAL OPPOSITION AND HOPELESSNESS. A message worth preaching!

We MUST therefore be willing to see people properly restored, *(with accountability and with much wisdom).* The following scripture reveals the exact attitude that God wants us to have towards RESTORATION:

*Brethren, if any person is overtaken in misconduct or sin of any sort, **you who are spiritual [who are responsive to and controlled by the Spirit]** should set him right and **RESTORE** AND **REINSTATE** HIM, without any sense of superiority and WITH ALL **GENTLENESS**, keeping an attentive eye on yourself, lest you should be tempted also.*

(Galatians 6:1)

❖

CHAPTER 5

The Holy Spirit
holds no Vendettas

Spiritual warfare could not be more real! We have all come under fire in one-way or another. In fact entire churches, its people and especially its leaders, all get "hit" at times. Some sadly never recover. YET it's the very heart of God that we do RECOVER, "…and they will RECOVER" *(Mark 16:18)*.

The Holy Spirit has no vendettas. There might be the wrath of the Lamb and of Almighty God, but let me say, nowhere in scripture does it speak of the wrath of the Spirit. His fruits are, love, joy, peace, kindness etc. He has FIRE and POWER – but not wrath, instead the Holy Spirit places God's love in our hearts.

FORGIVENESS, THE KEY TO REVIVAL

Such hope never disappoints or deludes or shames us, for **GOD'S <u>LOVE</u> HAS BEEN POURED OUT IN OUR HEARTS THROUGH THE HOLY SPIRIT** *Who has been given to us.*

(Romans 5:5)

The Spirit God gave us does not make us afraid. **HIS SPIRIT IS A SOURCE... <u>LOVE</u>.**

(2 Timothy 1:7 ERV)

With this in mind it is vital we "KNOW OF WHAT SORT OF SPIRIT WE ARE!" Satan is the accuser of the brethren who steals, kills and destroys. We must avoid common ground with any such negatives and line our thinking up with God's.

He sent messengers before Him; and they reached and entered a Samaritan village to make [things] ready for Him; But [the people] would not welcome or receive or accept Him... when His disciples James and John observed this, they said, Lord, **do You wish us to command fire to come down from heaven and consume them,** *even as Elijah did? But He turned and rebuked and severely censured them. He said,* **YOU DO NOT KNOW OF WHAT SORT OF SPIRIT YOU ARE,** *for the Son of Man did not come to destroy men's lives, but to save them [from the penalty of eternal death].*

(Luke 9:40-60)

This is such a vital point. Where there is zero forgiveness, it is impossible for a right spirit to be in operation. We are "known" by our fruits the bible states, so unforgiveness and bitterness should never be used to define "Born Again, Spirit Filled Believers," *(Oh how we have all fallen short on this one!)*

> *Master, we saw a man driving out demons in Your name and we commanded him to stop it, for he does not follow along with us. But Jesus told him,* **DO NOT FORBID [SUCH PEOPLE]; FOR WHOEVER IS NOT AGAINST YOU IS FOR YOU."**
>
> *(Luke 9:49-50)*

This scripture in Luke 9:49-50 strikes at the very heart of "competitiveness" in the ministry! I discovered long ago that BEING-RIGHT-IS-HIGHLY-OVER-RATED! In fact if being right is all that interests us, we have sadly developed SPIRITUAL PRIDE!

Now I want to address our opening scripture from chapter one, in Luke chapter 6 once again, using the Amplified version this time. Interestingly if we follow on a little and read the subsequent verse 38, it directly connects the concept of forgiveness with generosity and the release of plenty in our lives! Obviously then, forgiveness lifts the blockades in more ways than one!

Let me say, for those experiencing such "blockages" in various areas of their lives and ministry, that it is crucial they understand that no amount of "RELEASE" will happen without first addressing this major area of forgiveness. And let me add, that it is all too easy teaching about forgiveness when it remains a BLIND SPOT in our own lives!

Having judgmental attitudes, making negative remarks about others and unforgiveness can cause a strangle hold that no amount of spiritual warfare or prayer can unlock.

Sin in our own hearts cannot be prayed against. It requires repentance. In fact sometimes the quickest way to experience a release or a breakthrough, in any area, is via repentance.

In a small article that I read recently called **"The Rewards of Repentance"** *(p4)* Pat Robertson wrote:

How amazing to think that God completely cleanses us from our sins! The key is found in 1 John 1:9; **"IF WE CONFESS OUR SINS, HE IS FAITHFUL AND JUST TO FORGIVE US OUR SINS AND TO <u>CLEANSE</u> US FROM ALL UNRIGHTEOUSNESS"** *(NKJV).*

We have all done things worthy of condemnation, and the world certainly takes delight in condemning us. But Romans 8:1 promises, "There is therefore now no condemnation to those who are in Christ Jesus" *(NKJV).*

God doesn't dig up the past, and neither should we. "As far as the east is from the west, so far has He removed our transgressions from us" *(Psalm 103:12 NKJV).*

Hebrews 9:14 says, **"The blood of Christ will cleanse your conscience from dead works to serve the living God"** *(NKJV).* He forgives us completely so our conscience is clean and we can serve Him.

IF WE TRY TO COVER UP OUR SIN, HOWEVER, WE ARE ROBBED OF JOY AND <u>REVIVAL</u>. After David confesses his sin in Psalm 51, he says: "Make me hear joy and gladness... Restore to me the joy of Your salvation... Then I will teach transgressors Your ways, and sinners shall be converted to You" *(vv. 8, 12-13 NKJV).*

WHEN WE REPENT, WE RECEIVE FORGIVENESS, CLEANSING, SALVATION AND RIGHTEOUSNESS. This is our heritage in the Lord – and this is why Christians have joy! His Word promises, "No good thing will He withhold from those who walk uprightly" *(Psalm 84:11 NKJV)*.

There is a great move of God, and we are part of it. He wants us to be free from guilt and shame so we can experience His love and share it with others, drawing the world unto Him *(Pat Robertson)*.

❖

CHAPTER 6

The Boomerang Effect

Going through the motions using spiritual-rhetoric is also quite easy, we even seem to get away with it at first! But if we truly want to have impact and power operating through our lives, then we must follow biblical principles and instructions:

> *Leave your gift there before the altar and go. First be reconciled to your brother, and then come and offer your gift.*
> *(Matthew 5:24 ESV)*

In other words, our gifts and service are a complete waste of time when unforgiveness is present.

FORGIVENESS, THE KEY TO REVIVAL

Negative attitudes and comments are always corrosive. We must clean-up-the-spout, publicly and privately. Salt water and spring cannot flow out of the same place. *"Out of the same mouth proceedeth blessing and cursing. My brethren, these things ought not so to be"* (James 3:10 KJV).

Judge not [neither pronouncing judgment nor subjecting to censure], and you will not be judged; **do not condemn *and* pronounce guilty, and you will not be condemned *and* pronounced guilty; acquit *and* forgive *and* release (give up resentment, LET IT DROP), and you will be acquitted *and* forgiven *and* RELEASED.**

(Luke 6:37)

Verse 38 reads:

Give, and it shall be given to you; good measure, pressed, and shaken, and running over, they shall give into your bosom; **FOR WITH THAT MEASURE WITH WHICH YE MEASURE, IT SHALL BE MEASURED TO YOU AGAIN.**

(Luke 6:37 YLT)

This then is an undeniable fact, proving that our dealings with others, *(the measure that we use)* will rebound *(in due time)*, whether for good or for bad, big or small.

IN OTHER WORDS, WE DON'T GET AWAY WITH ANYTHING! Nothing we do goes unnoticed by heaven (Malachi 3:16). Whether word or deed, whether generous or stingy, behaviours good or bad *(ouch!)* The only thing that can break such a cycle is repentance.

In keeping with this particular subject, let's say it this way: **WE SIMPLY CANNOT DISENGAGE FROM "FORGIVENESS" AND STILL HOPE TO FUNCTION SUCCESSFULLY.** There is simply no biblical pretext for it.

The Message bible uses the word "boomerang" quite aptly:

> *Don't pick on people, jump on their failures, criticize their faults - unless, of course, you want the same treatment. Don't condemn those who are down; THAT HARDNESS CAN <u>BOOMERANG</u>. Be easy on people; you'll find life a lot easier. Give away your life; you'll find life given back, but not merely given back - given back with bonus and blessing. Giving, not getting, is the way. Generosity begets generosity."*
>
> *(Luke 6:37-38 MSG)*

❖

CHAPTER 7

This is a New Day!

In the King James Version of the bible, Hebrews 10:18 uses the word REMISSION instead of FORGIVENESS as used beneath. REMISSION refers to the "cancellation of the penalty" as can be seen in the Amplified Version.

I WILL ERASE THEIR SINS AND WICKED ACTS OUT OF MY MEMORY AS THOUGH THEY HAD NEVER EXISTED. When there is FORGIVENESS such as this, there is no longer any need to make an offering for sin.

(Hebrews 10:17-18 VOICE)

However let's go straight to the Greek by using the Strong's Concordance and see what it says about REMISSION.

FORGIVENESS, THE KEY TO REVIVAL

Greek #0859. αφεσισ aphesis; from 863; freedom; *(figuratively)* pardon: deliverance, forgiveness, liberty, and remission. AV *(17)*- remission 9, forgiveness 6, deliverance 1, liberty 1; **RELEASE FROM BONDAGE** or imprisonment, forgiveness or pardon, of sins *(LETTING THEM GO AS IF THEY HAD NEVER BEEN COMMITTED)*, remission of the penalty Greek #0860.

"RELEASE FROM BONDAGE... PARDON OF SINS *(LETTING THEM GO AS IF THEY HAD NEVER BEEN COMMITTED)*." Thank God such a condition exists. We could never achieve this status alone! If we take this to heart we can say: *"I am justified... just-as-if-I'd-never-sinned... whoop!"* Which is worthy of a party right there. What could be better! This is why we worship Jesus Christ in all of His Glory so vehemently and forever!

In keeping with our text I want to say, that it is not possible to express just how important forgiveness is. But we can try! Many times, we find ourselves in some form of spiritual warfare or another. However I firmly believe that much of the "fight" would swiftly diminish with the simple act of repentance *(with this I am also implying on a daily basis)*.

Today some camps exist who would deplore this idea, as being "sin conscious" and would argue that we aught to be more "righteous conscious." Absolutely! However when the day arrives where we no longer "repent" simply because we are trying to be "oh-so-righteous-conscious" *(when some folks can't even say it, let alone live it!)* then error has already crept into the Church. THERE NEVER HAS OR EVER WILL BE AN ADEQUATE REPLACEMENT FOR REPENTANCE.

YES Jesus' work on the cross was not inept; it was a complete and finished work of perfection. Even so, repentance was never done away with. Sophisticates in the Church today may want us to demean repentance and forgiveness – but they are both vital keys that unlock doors of bondage in all of our lives. We should never stumble at such truths but run to them gladly and with humility.

> *If we [freely] admit that we have sinned **and** confess our sins, He is faithful and just (true to His own nature and promises) and will FORGIVE our sins [dismiss our lawlessness] and [continuously] cleanse us from all unrighteousness [everything not in conformity to His will in purpose, thought, and action].*
>
> *(1 John 1:9)*

Once a person has sincerely repented they MUST move on, free of all condemnation:

> *THEREFORE, NOW **NO CONDEMNATION** AWAITS THOSE WHO ARE LIVING IN JESUS THE ANOINTED, **THE LIBERATING KING,** because when you live in the Anointed One, Jesus, a new law takes effect. The law of the Spirit of life breathes into you and liberates you from the law of sin and death.*
>
> *(Romans 8:1-2 VOICE)*

To stay in the realm of condemnation, when you know Christ has forgiven you, is really wilful unbelief! Instead we must allow the CONVICTION of the Holy Spirit to prick our hearts; this leads us to repentance, *(where condemnation only leads us to depression!)* Conviction is not the same as condemnation.

It's vital to recognize the difference between the two. It's equally as vital to know that the Holy Spirit NEVER condemns anyone. He convicts only. The devil on the other hand never stops accusing and condemning, *(especially believers)*. *"THE ACCUSER OF OUR **BRETHREN,** WHO **ACCUSED** THEM BEFORE OUR GOD **DAY AND NIGHT...** " (Revelation 12:10 KJV)*

Once again, if we are aware of this, we must never operate on any common ground with the devil. We must remember that ANY TIME WE ACCUSE OUR BROTHERS IN CHRIST, WE ARE STANDING ON THE SAME SIDE AS THE DEVIL. We must take sides with God and with His righteousness. We must be careful who we side-with! There is never a right time to accuse anyone. Especially other believers, *"the brethren."*

Touch not mine anointed, and do my prophets no harm.
(1 Chronicles 16:22 KJV)

Let not then your good be evil spoken of (slander)...
(Romans 14:16-18 NKJV)

I've heard this particular statement *(and similar versions of it)* branded around for many years, it goes something like this: **"I LOVE GOD AND WILL NEVER QUIT BELIEVING IN HIM, BUT I'VE ALREADY GIVEN UP ON THE CHURCH."** Now all of us would understand a statement like this. However, we must not be enticed into speaking badly about the Body of Christ, no matter how angry we get or how much injustice we have witnessed behind her walls.

Some folks are angry with the leadership, others are angry with the worship team and others with the children's ministry. But Jesus has not given up on His Bride yet and nor should we! He is coming back for her, without spot or wrinkle. She is going to have to go through a refining process to reach that stage of beauty. In the meantime we must not speak badly of the Church.

We must not take sides with the "accuser of the brethren," no matter how tempting this can be at times! WE ARE NOT A MOUTH PIECE FOR THE ACCUSER – WE ARE A MOUTH PIECE FOR GOD AND HIS TRUTH. Nor are we self-appointed mouthpieces for our own opinions! We should only speak when God directs.

IMPORTANT!
THE "WORDS" USED BY CHRISTIAN BELIEVERS ARE MANY TIMES MORE POWERFUL THAN THOSE OF A WITCHDOCTOR.

I want believers all over the world to understand, that their words are far more powerful than those of any witch-doctor, anywhere! This might come as a surprise to some folks even though scripture is very clear about this. We are all capable of blessing or cursing, of releasing life or death. We cannot deny scripture!

When God spoke, "MY PEOPLE perish for the lack of knowledge" He was referring to believers NOT unbelievers. Words can do irreparable damage or bring encouragement and life.

With the tongue we praise our Lord and Father, and with it we curse human beings, who have been made in God's likeness. **Out of the same mouth come praise and cursing.** *My brothers and sisters, this should not be.*

(James 3:9-10 NIV)

Ironically *this same tongue can be* **both an instrument** *of blessing to our Lord and Father and* **a weapon** *that hurls curses upon others who are created in God's own image. One mouth streams forth both* **blessings and curses.** *My brothers and sisters, this is not how it should be.*

(James 3:9-10 VOICE)

This is scary: You can tame a tiger, but you can't tame a tongue - it's never been done. **The tongue runs wild, a wanton killer.** *With our tongues we* **bless** *God our Father; with the same tongues we* **curse** *the very men and women he made in his image.* **CURSES AND BLESSINGS OUT OF THE SAME MOUTH!**

My friends, this can't go on. *A spring doesn't gush fresh water one day and brackish the next, does it? Apple trees don't bear strawberries, do they? Raspberry bushes don't bear apples, do they?* **You're not going to dip into a polluted mud hole and get a cup of clear, cool water, are you?**

(James 3:9-12 MSG)

This is why I said that the words of believers are more powerful than those of a witchdoctor. Some believers might not want to be placed in that same category. The only way to avoid such comparison is TO BLESS AND NEVER CURSE. Our mouths must be filled with His Grace, Love and to encourage ONLY.

This is a tremendous discipline, which only God can achieve in us. As the scripture has already stated, *"You can tame a tiger,* **but you can't tame a tongue - it's never been done.** *The tongue runs wild, a wanton killer."*

The only solution is to yield our tongues to God; He alone has the ability to tame our tongues – from the inside out – through His Holy Spirit abiding in us, with power to change our hearts.

❖

CHAPTER 8

The Root
of Bitterness

In my book called **"Deliverance a Present Reality"** *(p135-136)* which was written many years ago now, I explained about the role that BITTERNESS plays along with its crippling effect on the lives of so many people. I am happy to say that we can be FREE of bitterness and its influence BUT only through the power of forgiveness!

*See to it that no one falls short of the grace of God and that **no BITTER ROOT GROWS UP TO CAUSE TROUBLE AND DEFILE MANY.***

(Hebrews 12:15 NIV)

No bitter root should be allowed to grow within our lives, but the fact is that many of us at some time have been bruised. We had the experience of falling from a tree like an apple;

at first the shock of bouncing to the ground was deflected, shaken off. But some days or months later the bruise began to show, like an apple we begin to rot with bitterness. We poison ourselves and everyone who surrounds us, because of our attitudes and the things that we begin to say.

Others pick up *(or transferred)* the bitterness that we have and then they too become polluted. We want to blame other people because we have become bitter. The bitterness then becomes hatred. This then is the opening that Satan uses to afflict us with evil spirits and diseases. For those who have been bitter or unforgiving over the years, sometimes it expresses itself in crippling arthritis or other manifestations. The remedy, forgiveness towards those who have hurt us, for whatever reason, needs to take place. Then healing can be brought about.

Forgiveness is the key to release bitterness, resentments and other negative emotions. We need not judge or condemn others for in so doing we will not be condemned. "Forgive and you will be forgiven" *(Luke 6:37)*.

If we are not willing to forgive, forgiveness will not come our way. We have been forgiven of sin; our debt has been cancelled; yet we find it hard to forgive others *(Matthew 18:27)*. We need to release our brothers and sisters from whatever they have done towards us. If we do not forgive we will become like them. The end result of unforgiveness is that we will be turned over to the jailer *(or remain in the jailer's camp)* to be tortured *(Matthew 18:34)*.

Forgiveness is the attitude of God and the example that we must follow. We might not feel like forgiving, but then we cannot go on feelings, we need to be obedient to the Word of God. Forgiveness then becomes an act of the will, when we choose to forgive: *"If you forgive men when they sin against you, your heavenly Father will also forgive you. But **IF YOU DO NOT FORGIVE MEN THEIR SINS, YOUR FATHER WILL NOT FORGIVE YOUR SINS"** (Matthew 6:14-15 NIV)."*

Now notice in each case where the scriptures below mention forgiveness, it directly connects forgiveness with the HEART. Forgiveness is always a heart issue. We must therefore, *"guard our hearts above all else"* (Proverbs 4:23 NLT).

*In wrath his master turned him over to the torturers (the jailers), till he should pay all that he owed. **So also My heavenly Father will deal with every one of you if you do not <u>FREELY FORGIVE YOUR BROTHER FROM YOUR HEART</u> his offenses.***

(Matthew 18:34-35)

*His master's **HEART** was moved with compassion, and he **<u>RELEASED</u>** him and **<u>FORGAVE</u>** him [cancelling] the debt.*

(Matthew 18:27)

Let's just revisit the scripture that was briefly mentioned above, this time pointing out the heart-mouth connection. The heart-mouth connection is also a major part of forgiveness. Here I have taken various translations and allowed them to speak for themselves:

ABOVE ALL ELSE, WATCH OVER YOUR HEART; *diligently guard it because from a sincere and pure heart come the good and noble things of life. **Do away with***

*any talk that twists and distorts the truth; have
nothing to do with any verbal trickery.*

(*Proverbs 4:23-24 VOICE*)

*ABOVE EVERY CHARGE KEEP THY HEART, for
out of it [are] the outgoings of life.*

(*Proverbs 4:23 YLT*)

*KEEP VIGILANT WATCH OVER YOUR HEART;
that's where life starts. Don't talk out of both sides of
your mouth...*

(*Proverbs 4:23 MSG*)

*It's the same with people. A person full of goodness in
his heart produces good things; a person with an evil
reservoir in his heart pours out evil things. THE HEART
OVERFLOWS IN THE WORDS A PERSON
SPEAKS; YOUR WORDS REVEAL WHAT'S
WITHIN YOUR HEART.*

(*Luke 6:45 VOICE*)

❖

CHAPTER 9

Destiny is in Your Mouth

Our Faith should be our profession. God never does anything without saying it first! God is a faith God. God released His faith in Words. *"...Have faith in God"* (Mark 11:22 NIV). Literally meaning, *"Have the God kind of faith"* or *"Have the faith of God."*

Ephesians 5:1 tells us to be imitators of God as children imitate their parents. To imitate God, you must talk like Him and act like Him. He would not ask you to do something you are not capable of doing.

Jesus operated in the faith principles of Mark 11:23, and Matthew 17:20 while He was on earth. He *spoke* to the wind and sea. He *spoke* to demons. He *spoke* to the fig tree. He even *spoke* to dead men!

God released His faith in His Words. Jesus was imitating His Father and getting the same results. In John 14:12 Jesus said, *"…He that believeth on me the works that I do shall he do also; and greater…" (KJV)* These principles of faith are based on spiritual laws that work for whosoever applies them and sets them in motion by the words that they speak.

If Jesus came to you personally today and said, "As of today whatsoever you say will directly come to pass, exactly as you have said it…" You would appropriate some real quick changes wouldn't you!

Words are like seeds, they produce after their own kind. Faith comes more quickly when you hear yourself quoting, speaking, and saying the things God said. You will more readily receive God's Word into your spirit by hearing yourself say it than if you hear someone else say it. *(Romans 10:17)*

Better watch what we say! Much of what the Father supplies to the Body of Christ is *furnished through our confession.* This is not simply our positive, premeditated confession expressed in prayer; it consists of *everything* that comes out of our mouths.

Spoken words program our hearts and minds for success or defeat and our words are the overflow of the condition of our hearts. Christ, as the *"High Priest of our confession" (Hebrews 3:1 NASB),* takes our words, whether in faith or unbelief, and allocates back to us eternal life in proportion to our words. When our tongue is unbridled, James tells us that our negative confession *"...sets on fire the course of our life, and is set on fire by hell" (James 3:6 NASB).*

In Hebrews 3:1 we are instructed to, *"Consider the apostle and high Priest of our profession Christ Jesus" (KJV).* The word translated as **"profession"** in that verse can also be translated as **"confession."** God appointed and anointed Jesus to be high priest over our confession or profession *(lit. our words of faith).*

Jesus brings our words to pass. 1 Corinthians 1:4-5 also tells us that Jesus *...enriches* our utterance. That is, He takes our words of faith and enriches them with His Anointing. So no matter how we look at it, the words we speak carry the very creative force of Almighty God behind them. They will come to pass!

We are created to be the *prophet of our own lives!* Our destiny is in our mouths. It's our words - not everyone else's - that determine our success, or failure, in this life *(Romans 10:8-9).* Our words can bring either good or evil things into our lives.

*Out of the abundance of the heart **the mouth speaks.** A good man out of the good treasure of his heart brings forth **good things,** and an evil man out of the evil treasure brings forth **evil things.***

(Matthew 12:34-37 KJV)

The different kinds of confession are as follows. The Confession of Sin [prior to the Cross]: Prior to Jesus going to the cross, *John the Baptist and Jesus taught confession of sin* *to the Jewish people.* The Jews knew what it was to confess their sins and repent, but their sins were only *"covered"* in atonement by the blood of an animal which was sacrificed once a year. It wasn't until the sacrifice of Jesus' blood that sin could actually be wiped out and not just covered up *(see Hebrews 10).*

The Confession unto Salvation [post-Cross]: This is the confession of a sinner, known as the prayer of salvation. In John 16, when Jesus told His disciples about the soon coming Holy Spirit, He explained that the Spirit would come to convict *"the world"* of sin. But what were these *"sinners"* to do, once convicted by the Spirit?

Romans 10:8-9 *(KJV)* tells us;

The word is nigh thee, even in thy mouth, *and in thy heart: that is, the word of faith, which we preach; that if thou shalt confess with thy mouth the Lord Jesus, and shalt believe in thine heart that God hath raised Him from the dead, thou shalt be saved.*

Basically, the confession of a sinner under the New Covenant is simply this: **"Jesus Christ is Lord!"**

The Saint's Confession: Today, the Church is full of Christians who have no idea how to confess their sins once they do step out of fellowship with the Father - which is our third New Testament confession.

The bible says, if you <u>have</u> sin in your life, get it out - confess it, repent of it, get rid of it. Once you do, stand on 1 John 1:9, which says, *"If we* **confess our sins,** *he is faithful* and just to forgive us our sins, and to cleanse us from all unrighteousness" (NIV).

According to 1 John 1 & 2, when we as believers are out of fellowship with the Father - that is, when we sin - we know it. That's the time to get rid of it. *Immediately!* After all, 1 John 2:1 assures us that, *"If any man sin, we have an advocate with the Father, Jesus Christ the righteous" (KJV).* Don't run from Him when you sin, *Run to Him.*

The moment we confessed our sin is the moment we got rid of it. By faith, we *spewed it out* of our mouths and God was faithful and just to forgive us and cleanse us.

Confession of our Faith in Christ: Found in the New Testament is the confession of our faith in God's Word, our faith in Christ - or His Anointing - our faith in God the Father, and our faith in the faithfulness of Jesus as our High Priest.

Remember whatever you and I receive from God, we receive it by confession. *Your Mouth is "the Master Key to Life."*

The apostle Paul wrote to the Hebrews:

Consider the Apostle and High Priest of our confession Christ Jesus.

(Hebrews 3:1 KJV)

The word *"confession"* in the Greek actually means, *"saying the same thing as (or) saying what God says."*

• It's the affirmation of a bible truth, which one is particularly embracing, *(or...)*

59

• Repeating with the lips, the thing that God has said in His Word, which is also believed in the heart.

What you Feed, you BREAD
& What you Starve Dies...!

A good man eats good from the fruit of his mouth, but the desire of the treacherous is for violence. He who guards his mouth keeps his life, but he who opens wide his lips comes to ruin.

(Proverbs 13:2-3)

Our confessions - the words we constantly speak day after day - determine all that we will ever receive from God, whether it's salvation, physical healing, peace or financial prosperity. What's more, for the rest of our eternal existence, *this principle of faith working hand in hand with our confession will never change.*

Looking once more at faith: In Mark 11:23 *(KJV)* Jesus explained how that faith process works;

*Whoever shall **say** unto this mountain, Be thou removed, and be thou cast into the sea; and shall not doubt in his heart, but shall believe that those things which he **saith** shall come to pass; he shall have whatsoever he **saith**.*

Faith operates by believing and saying and saying and saying. It is our confession, or words of faith, that brings possession. We saw that in Romans 10:10 *"With the heart man believeth...and with the mouth confession is made unto..." (KJV)* And in Matthew 12:34-35, *"Out of the abundance of the heart the mouth speaketh..." (KJV)*

We lay hold of the word by receiving it by faith, and then *confessing* it. **This same process got us saved and it's this process that will get us anything else God has promised!** Remember, once we lay hold of the promises of God with our faith and our confession that's when Jesus' enriching Anointing and ministry come into play.

That's why the Apostle Paul told Timothy that, *"Words of faith"* nourish, but idle words starve the spirit and make it weak *(1 Timothy 4:6-7)*.

So we must, *"Hold fast the profession of our faith..."* It is our **CONFESSION** of faith, which makes the difference between life or death.

❖

CHAPTER 10

Seduction
Brings Bondage

Referring again to my book **"Deliverance a Present Reality"** *(published in 1994)* in the chapter called "Entry Points for Demonic Influences" I wrote the following *(p120-122):*

God's intention is that we enjoy life, but how can we enjoy life if we are not taking responsibility in regards to those in authority. When a person rebels, he is walking in sin *(Romans 13:1-7)*. This in turn, if prolonged, will leave the door open for Satan to afflict him with his evil desires, which is to totally lead man astray.

A man or woman then who will not take seriously God's given authority will begin to become a slave to the temptation and the deceptions of his own body. He will believe the series of the flesh, the perversion and fantasy of the mind, and be led into deception. We need to be careful not to become slaves to sin, for this can lead to death.

> *Don't you know that when you offer yourselves to someone to obey him as slaves, you are slaves to the one whom you obey - whether you are slaves to sin, which leads to death, or to obedience which leads to righteousness? But thanks be to God that, though you used to be slaves to sin, you wholeheartedly obeyed the form of teaching to which you were entrusted.*

Sin then, is a choice, and if not dealt with can become a habit, which in turn will lead to bondage. Open doors give evil spirits the opportunity to tempt, deceive, accuse, condemn, pressure, defile, resist, oppose, control, steal, afflict, kill and destroy. The only way to be free of Satan and his evil devices is to receive Jesus Christ as Lord and Saviour.

But for many Christians it would seem even after their born-again experience, rebellion still needs to be dealt with. Sometimes it would seem that this can only be done by being turned over to the flesh, for we need to crucify the sinful nature *(Galatians 5:19-21)*. If this action is not taken by us then it will be taken by God. For... *"as obedient children, do not conform to the evil desires you had when you lived in ignorance. But just as he who called you is holy, so be holy in all you do; for it is written: Be holy, because I am holy"* *(1 Peter 1:15-16 NIV)*.

Failure to turn from our rebellious ways can only result in us being delivered into the hands of Satan, so that the sinful nature - the flesh - can be destroyed and the spirit man saved *(1 Corinthians 1-5)*. Sin has dramatic results upon our lives. Doors that have been open by sin can affect our lives for many years.

In the same book I also discuss many other entry points that Satan can use in order to gain a foothold or stronghold; such as emotional traumas, grief, miscarriage, ancestry blood lines, curses and rejection. *(BUT you are just going to have to get the book!)*

However when it comes to sin, how do people really fall into it? Very often this is done through means of seduction. Just like in the Garden of Eden and the very first sin, if you like, it was the seduction of the snake that caused Eve to step out of alignment with God and with her husband. She stepped out of her ordained role of "help meet" and began to "help-herself!" *(Genesis 2:18 KJV)*

In the King James Version it says it the best because it puts the responsibility right where it belongs, *"Every man is tempted, when he is drawn away of his OWN lust, and enticed"* *(James 1:14 KJV)*. In this context there is no blaming God or the devil, but self!

In various other translations it reads like so:

*But every person is tempted when he is drawn away, enticed and **baited by his own evil desire** (lust, passions).*

(AMP)

*Don't let anyone under pressure to give in to evil say, "God is trying to trip me up." God is impervious to evil, and puts evil in no one's way. **The temptation to give*** *in to evil comes from us and only us. We have no one to blame but the leering, seducing flare-up of our OWN lust. Lust gets pregnant, and has a baby: sin! Sin grows up to adulthood, and becomes a real killer.*

(James 1:13-15 MSG)

Scripture puts the onus on us, where it belongs. People evidently don't just step into sin without warning. There is a process. *"The seducing flare-up of our own lust"* is something that takes place over a period of time. Each time they choose not to restrain themselves, their lusts were further ignited instead. But we must remember that sin is only pleasurable *"for a season" (Hebrews 11:25 KJV).*

I saw this written on a poster, **"SIN FASCINATES, THEN ASSASSINATES,"** which is a fairly good analogy because that's pretty much the process involved.

God always gives us time to repent. Even Jezebel: *"I have given her time to repent of her immorality, but she is unwilling" (Revelation 2:21 NIV).*

It takes time to percolate coffee! Likewise it takes time to become impregnated with lust. *"Lust gets pregnant, and has a baby: sin! Sin grows up to adulthood, and becomes a real killer" (James 1:13-15 MSG).*

Sin takes time to get "established." By the time it does, we are hooked. The bondage has a firm footing and strongholds are always in it for keeps! Satan comes to steel, kill and destroy, three definitive roles. Though his strategy is usually to get us to self-destruct!

We don't need much encouragement to destroy our lives, especially if the conditions are pleasurable! We are creatures of comfort and habit. Easily given to self-love.

Self-preservation is a major part of any enticement. It involves our "right" to exercise some *(not self-control but)* self-indulgence! The flesh is selfish, and is blind to the long-term effect of our temporal lack of restraint.

> *Why do you let that Jezebel who calls herself a prophet mislead my dear servants into... self-indulging religion? ...I x-ray every motive and make sure you get what's coming to you.*
>
> *(Revelation 2:20-23 MSG)*

God will not be taken lightly:

> *Take heed to yourselves, lest you forget the covenant of the Lord your God which He made with you, and make for yourselves a graven image in the form of anything which the Lord your God has forbidden you.*
>
> *For the Lord your **GOD IS A CONSUMING FIRE**, a jealous God.*
>
> *(Deuteronomy 4:23-24)*

The process of sin and seduction is played out best in the example of adultery. It is not an instant thing that happens. It happens over TIME. No one just steps into bed with another person *(other than their own spouse)* it has taken a process of attraction and many moments of inward weakness, long before physical adultery takes place between the sheets!

You have heard that it was said, "You shall not commit adultery." But I tell you that anyone who **LOOKS** *at a woman lustfully* **HAS ALREADY COMMITTED ADULTERY WITH HER IN HIS HEART.**

(Matthew 5:27-28 NIV)

You know the next commandment pretty well, too: "Don't go to bed with another's spouse." But don't think you've preserved your virtue simply by staying out of bed. **YOUR HEART CAN BE CORRUPTED BY LUST EVEN QUICKER THAN YOUR BODY.** *Those leering looks you think nobody notices - they also corrupt.*

(MSG)

❖

CHAPTER 11

The Great Decline

In his book **"Protection from Deception"** *(p50-55)* Derek Prince outlines the *"three steps of decline"* from true Godly wisdom. Once we take our eyes from God's wisdom, we enter a very fast decline indeed!

This wisdom descendeth not from above, but is **EARTHLY, SENSUAL, DEVILISH.**

(James 3:15 KJV)

Let's take a look at what he says on this important issue: James 3:15 is pithy yet profound, ***"This wisdom does not descend from above, but is earthly, sensual, demonic"*** *(NKJV)*. This passage marks the steps in the decline of wisdom, a decline that allows demons to infiltrate the work, people, and the Church of God. Being earthly may seem innocent enough, but it takes little time for apathy to take root, dragging the individual down into the soulish realm, and perhaps further still into the realm of the demonic.

What does it mean to be *earthly?* From a Christian standpoint, *earthly* individuals focus on our *earthly* life and nothing more – nothing beyond. If an *earthly* individual is a Christian, he expects God to provide blessings applicable only to this lifetime: prosperity, healing, power, success, and other *soulish* pursuits.

To gain a better understanding of the *earthly* individual, it is useful to recognize individuals who were decidedly *unearthly.*

One such example is Abraham:

By faith he dwelt in the land of promise as in a foreign country, dwelling in tents with Isaac and Jacob, the heirs with him of the same promise; for he waited for the city, which has foundations, whose builder and maker is God.
(Hebrews 11:9-10 NKJV)

Abraham accepted the temporality of *earthly* life, dwelling in a tent instead of building a residence in the Promised Land. By contrast, Lot, who separated from Abraham and turned toward the wicked town of Sodom, lived in a house and abandoned an *eternal mind-set* for a mundane one.

God expects us to adopt Abraham's mind-set. This world is not our home. When we forget that, we become *soulish.*

A second example of an *unearthly* individual was Moses, described in Hebrews 11:27, *"By faith he forsook Egypt, not fearing the wrath of the king; for he endured as seeing Him who is invisible" (NKJV).* **Moses endured because he looked past the present hardships to the certainty of future fulfillment.**

In 1 Corinthians 15:9, Paul wrote, *"If in this life only we have hope in Christ, we are of all men the most pitiable" (NKJV).* If the purpose of our Christian faith is to receive blessings in this earthly life alone, we are to be pitied. Many have forgotten the fact that we are foreigners passing through this world, and consequently, their thoughts and ambitions lose proper focus. **They have become *earthly*.**

Soulish is the level below earthly. What is the essence of the soul? As described previously, the soul is essentially the ego. *Soulish* people are egocentric, concerned exclusively with themselves.

While the spiritual person asks, **"How can I glorify God?"** the *soulish* person asks, **"What's in it for me?"** The contemporary church caters too often to this quest of personal gain instead of God's glory.

In 1 Corinthians 2:14-15 *(NKJV)*, Paul wrote,

*But the natural **[soulish]** man does not receive the things of the Spirit of God, for they are foolishness to him; nor can he know them, because they are spiritually discerned. But he who is spiritual judges all things, yet he himself is rightly judged by no one.*

The *soulish* man cannot discern spiritual truth because he must do so with the spirit; he is attuned solely to *soulish* appeals to his emotions. One can be motivated by *soulishness* to contribute a substantial tithe and/or offering to the church, but this improper motivation will render it ineffectual.

Soulish people worship God in order to have a good time. "Wonderful worship service," they often say. But the purpose of worship is not for us to have a good time. Rather, the purpose of worship is just what it says – worship! **Proper worship praises God; it does not seek to elevate our emotions or to thrill our senses.** In the process of worshipping God, our emotions may or may not be elevated or thrilled, but this should not be our primary focus.

Having been a preacher for many years, I have seen *soulish* appeals to emotions that move people to tears and make them excited – without changing them. One week later, they are usually the same. **It is lamentable how many churches specialize in the realm of the soul rather than in the realm of the spirit.** People in the *soulish* realm are carried away with little effort, setting themselves up for deception. **This can be avoided only distinguishing between the spiritual and the *soulish* realm.**

A step down from *soulish* is the *demonic.* The pattern of progression from *earthly* to *soulish* to **demonic** is perhaps best illustrated in the Old Testament by Aaron, a high priest of Israel who fashioned a golden idol. Exodus 32:1-6 *(NKJV)* describes his decline:

Now when the people saw that Moses delayed coming down from the mountain, the people gathered together to

*Aaron, and said to him, "Come, make us **gods** that shall go before us; for as for this Moses, **the MAN who brought us up out of the land of Egypt,** we do not know what has become of him."*

And Aaron said to them, "Break off the golden earrings which are in the ears of your wives, your sons, and your daughters, and bring them to me." So all the people broke off the golden earrings, which were in their ears, and brought them to Aaron. And he received the gold from their hand, and he fashioned it with an engraving tool, and made a molded calf.

*Then they said, **"THIS is your god, O Israel, that brought you out of the land of Egypt!"** So when Aaron saw it, he built an altar before it. And Aaron made a proclamation and said, "Tomorrow is a feast to the Lord [Yahweh]." Then they rose early on the next day, offered burnt offerings, and brought peace offerings; and **the people sat down to eat and drink, AND ROSE UP TO PLAY.***

There are several significant details in this passage to note. First the people credited Moses for the deliverance – "the man who brought us up out of the land of Egypt" – instead of recognizing God's providence. Their focus on human leaders turned into idolatry.

The passage concludes with idolatry, too – *"the people... rose up to play."* Play is the essence of idolatry, and when our worship becomes play, we have slipped from the spiritual to the *soulish,* and – ultimately – to the *demonic.*

Much of what we call "worship" in our churches is not worship at all. It is self-centered, focusing on finding out how to obtain God's healing, blessings, and other provisions. **Much music in today's church services appeals to the soul, stimulating it in the same way that secular music might.**

What is incredible about the backsliding of Aaron and the people is how suddenly it occurred. **TWO MONTHS BEFORE Aaron fashioned the golden calf, Moses received the Ten Commandments from God on Mount Sinai.** The people responded appropriately with awe, fear, and reverence, as Exodus 20:18-21 *(NKJV)* describes:

> *Now all the people witnessed the thunderings, the lightning flashes, the sound of the trumpet, and the mountain smoking; and when the people saw it, they trembled and stood afar off. Then they said to Moses, "You speak with us, and we will hear; but let not God speak with us, lest we die." And Moses said to the people, "Do not fear; for God has come to test you, and that His fear may be before you, SO THAT YOU MAY NOT SIN."*

Finally, Derek Prince concludes, with a challenge for each individual and every church doorstep worldwide:

WITHIN TWO MONTHS, THE PEOPLE HAD ABANDONED THEIR ATTITUDE OF FEAR AND REVERENCE, AND IN ITS PLACE WAS **AN ATTITUDE OF INDIFFERENCE AND IDOLATRY.** Once their physical needs had been met – their appetites sated, their bodies sufficiently clothed – **THEY DEMANDED ENTERTAINMENT IN THE FORM OF WORSHIP** *(Derek Prince).*

With this I will conclude by saying, evidently we are creatures of comfort, but first and foremost we were created to worship. This is demonstrated and proven by the fact, that even in our worst condition, we still gravitate towards worship. We instinctively know that we must worship "something" or "someone" even if it's ourselves.

Narcissism for example is prevalent throughout the world today *(extreme self-centeredness and self-worship)*, which is idolatry. To worship anything other than God is idolatry and rebellion. Young teens are encouraged to "idolize" their favourite celebrities, actors, singers and so on, and by so doing, help to create the very *lucrative* "teen-idol" phenomena. Making giant music moguls such as Simon Cowl *(creator of The X Factor and the British boy band, One Direction)* and Simon Fuller *(creator of American Idol, and the Spice Girls)* very, very wealthy individuals!

Here remains the challenge, for every individual believer and church around the world. No matter how great or how small in number. In order to avoid the errors, excesses and influences of the great decline: *(from earthly, soulish to demonic)* we must declare what Jesus stated in the wilderness: *"Thou shalt worship the Lord thy God, and him ONLY shalt thou serve" (KJV)*. Or as the Message bible wonderfully states: *"Worship the Lord your God, and only him. Serve him with ABSOLUTE SINGLE-HEARTEDNESS" (Matthew 4:10 MSG)*.

We must never leave the Glory. Wherever the Spirit of the Lord is, there is LIBERTY! *"Arise, shine; for they light is come and* **the GLORY of the Lord is risen upon thee...** *the Lord shall arise upon thee, and* **his GLORY shall be seen upon**

thee. *And the Gentiles shall come to thy light…" (Isaiah 60:1-3; 2 Corinthians 3:17 KJV)*

This chapter is about sin, but it is sin to worship anything other than God. To worship Him for what we can get rather than what we can give Him. In His presence is the fullness of joy, because God inhabits the praises of His people. We are undeniably blessed as we remain in His presence. But worship is all about Him and not about us.

❖

CHAPTER 12

The Spirit
of Discontent

This chapter must be included in this book about forgiveness; all about the spirit of discontent. So what happens when we become discontented?

She looks well to how things go in her household,
and the bread of idleness (gossip, discontent, and self-pity)
she will not eat.

(Proverbs 31:27)

Quite simply it breaks down the fabric of our lives. The spirit of discontent is a mean spirit that will not stop until we have lost everything. On the other hand, the Holy Spirit will ensure that we embrace a spirit of thankfulness:

In everything give thanks: for this is the will of God in Christ Jesus concerning you.

(1 Thessalonians 5:18 KJV)

Enter into his gates with thanksgiving, and into his courts with praise: be thankful unto him, and bless his name.

(Psalm 100:4 KJV)

Most of all:

Perverse disputings of men of corrupt minds, and destitute of the truth, supposing that gain is godliness: from such withdraw thyself. **BUT GODLINESS WITH CONTENTMENT IS GREAT GAIN.** *For we brought nothing into this world, and it is certain we can carry nothing out.*

(1 Timothy 6:5-7 KJV)

The blessing of the Lord, it maketh rich, and **HE ADDETH NO SORROW WITH IT.**

(Proverbs 10:22 KJV)

For women in general and wives in particular scripture says that they will desire their husbands and not despise them! The same is true vice-versa of course. Forgiveness is an integral part of the marriage union. Daily forgiveness! Marriage is not an automatic union! It takes much WORK!

We can't be led by our feelings or our appetites, the bible clearly states: "*Man shall not live by bread alone, but by every word that proceedeth out of the mouth of God*" (Matthew 4:4 KJV).

If the feelings of discontent have risen up, then possibly we've taken our eyes off of the Father God – whom we have trusted - and been deceived by our feelings that we now trust instead!

Do we trust feelings more than God? Most of what we are talking about will only be real revelation to us if we get back to developing our relationship with God. Joy comes from the Glory. In the presence of God is the fullness of joy!

If the joy has gone out of our marriages, then we need the presence back in our marriages! Once we trust Him and are bathed in His Glory we'll have faith for our circumstances to turn around along with our spouses to be transformed!

I love to utilize different translations of the bible. Reading the following scripture in various translations, reveals very clearly just how sanctification can take place in our most important family relationships *(our spouse and children)* if our behaviour and the words that we speak are sanctified:

For the unbelieving husband is sanctified by the wife, and the unbelieving wife is sanctified by the husband: else were your children unclean; but now are they holy.
(1 Corinthians 7:14 KJV)

For the Christian wife ***BRINGS HOLINESS TO HER MARRIAGE,*** *and* *the Christian husband* ***BRINGS HOLINESS TO HIS MARRIAGE.*** *Otherwise, your children would not be holy, but now they are holy.*
(NLT)

*For the unbelieving husband hath been **SANCTIFIED IN THE WIFE,** and the unbelieving wife hath **BEEN SANCTIFIED IN THE HUSBAND;** otherwise your children are unclean, but now they are holy.*

(YLT)

*Here's the reason: An unbelieving husband is **CONSECRATED BY THAT UNION - TOUCHED BY THE GRACE OF GOD** through his believing wife - and the same is true when the husband is a man of faith and he's wed to an unbelieving wife. His wife is **CONSECRATED THROUGH THEIR UNION.** If this weren't so, your children wouldn't be pure; but as it is **when faith enters in, God sets apart these children to be used uniquely for His purposes.***

(VOICE)

For the rest of you who are in mixed marriages - Christian married to non-Christian - we have no explicit command from the Master. So this is what you must do. If you are a man with a wife who is not a believer but who still wants to live with you, hold on to her. If you are a woman with a husband who is not a believer but he wants to live with you, hold on to him.

***THE UNBELIEVING HUSBAND SHARES TO AN EXTENT IN THE HOLINESS OF HIS WIFE,** and the unbelieving wife is likewise **TOUCHED BY THE HOLINESS OF HER HUSBAND.** Otherwise, your children would be left out; as it is, they also are included in the spiritual purposes of God.*

(MSG)

FOR THE UNBELIEVING HUSBAND IS SET APART (SEPARATED, WITHDRAWN FROM HEATHEN CONTAMINATION, AND AFFILIATED WITH THE CHRISTIAN PEOPLE) BY UNION WITH HIS CONSECRATED (SET-APART) WIFE, and the unbelieving wife is SET APART AND SEPARATED THROUGH UNION WITH HER CONSECRATED HUSBAND. Otherwise your children would be unclean (unblessed heathen, outside the Christian covenant), but as it is they are prepared for God [pure and clean].

(AMP)

This reminds me of Hebrews 12:14 *(KJV)* where it says: "Follow peace with all men, and **HOLINESS,** without which no man shall see the Lord," which in the Young's Literal Translation says: "Peace pursue with all, **AND THE SEPARATION,** apart from which no one shall see the Lord."

Quite simply, holiness in its simplest form, is SEPARATION unto God and a lifestyle that is SEPARATED unto God, will influence everyone and everything around us including our precious children.

*All thy children shall be taught of the Lord; and **GREAT SHALL BE THE PEACE OF THY CHILDREN.***

(Isaiah 54:13 KJV)

❖

CHAPTER 13

The Glory
Needs to Come Back

I purposely put this chapter towards the end of this book because it is of major importance to our lives. If we are going to be, believing-believers, with power and influence upon our lives! Not pitiful but powerful, like Jesus was in the earth. We simply must have the Glory flowing to and through our lives. Only then can we truly be effective. It's imperative that we believe for the Glory back.

Especially poignant for those who have been backslidden for a period of their lives and have become battle weary. The type of person who is asking right now: "How do I get the glory back in my life?"

FORGIVENESS, THE KEY TO REVIVAL

It has been said, **"THERE IS NO TORMENT, LIKE THE TORMENT THAT BELONGS TO THOSE WHO HAVE KNOWN GOD, HIS PRESENCE AND HIS GRACE, AND HAVE WALKED AWAY!"**

Let's turn to the Word to see what it says about the Glory of God being in our lives and the influence that it has, not only on the individual but also upon the nations!

> *Arise [from the depression and prostration in which circumstances have kept you - rise to a new life]!* **SHINE (BE RADIANT WITH THE GLORY OF THE LORD),** *for your light has come, and the glory of the Lord has risen upon you!*
>
> <u>*For behold, darkness shall cover the earth, and dense darkness*</u> *[all] peoples,* **BUT THE LORD SHALL ARISE UPON YOU... HIS GLORY SHALL BE SEEN ON YOU.**
>
> **THEN YOU SHALL SEE AND BE RADIANT,** *and* **your heart shall thrill and tremble with joy [at the glorious deliverance] and be enlarged; BECAUSE THE ABUNDANT WEALTH** *of the [Dead] Sea* **shall be turned to you,** *unto you shall the nations come with their treasures.*
>
> *(Isaiah 60:1-2, 5)*

This scripture is speaking of Jerusalem. But we have been grafted into this promise, it applies to us too, hallelujah! It talks of "dense darkness" covering the people. This reminds me of the Passover in Egypt when the darkness was tangible and where it could literally be "felt" *(see Exodus 10:21).*

Finally, it's time to be radiant because of His Glory upon our lives:

Arise, shine, for your light has broken through! **THE ETERNAL ONE'S <u>BRILLIANCE</u> HAS DAWNED UPON YOU...** *God will rise and shine on you; the Eternal's bright glory will shine on you, a light for all to see.*

(Isaiah 60:1-2 VOICE)

❖

CHAPTER 14

There is Life
after Every Mistake

It is "wilful" sin that we find hard to deal with. If we think that someone hurt us by mistake, then somehow it's easier to handle, but what about the premeditated stuff? What about the character assassination attempts, the slander that damages our hard earned credibility and the betrayal that takes place? "*A whisperer separateth chief friends*" *(Proverbs 16:28 KJV)*

Perverse people stir up contention; gossip makes best friends into enemies.

(Proverbs 16:28 VOICE)

Hard as it may be, we are obligated to forgive this too. How about our own wilfulness? All those times we knew

87

better and those times we didn't? However I am here to say that THERE IS LIFE AFTER EVERY MISTAKE.

Again how about those prominent TV personalities who have fallen from grace in spectacular fashion and in the midst of great controversy? What of them? Do we judge crudely like so many have, with no advanced knowledge of their circumstances? In the first chapter I mentioned Todd Bentley and the process of being restored back into the ministry. It took a great deal of repentance and forgiveness on all sides. However what I did not share is that he disclosed that Christians [YES! Christians] sent him shocking hate mail and even death threats! This is hard to believe and there is little that surprises me these days!

Romans 3:23 says, "All have sinned and fallen short." ALL means ALL in scripture, there is none who escapes no matter how good they think they have been. We were born into sin. Not a day goes by without some kind of mishap or other. Yet one vital prerequisite prevails, which Jesus taught in the famous formula that He gave to His disciples:

FORGIVE US OUR DEBTS, AS WE ALSO HAVE FORGIVEN (left, remitted, and let go of the debts, and have given up resentment against) our debtors... For IF you forgive people their trespasses [their reckless and willful sins, leaving them, letting them go, and giving up resentment], your heavenly Father will also forgive you. BUT IF YOU DO NOT FORGIVE OTHERS THEIR TRESPASSES [THEIR RECKLESS AND WILLFUL SINS, LEAVING THEM, LETTING THEM GO,

AND GIVING UP RESENTMENT], <u>NEITHER WILL YOUR FATHER FORGIVE YOU YOUR TRESPASSES</u>.

(Matthew 6:9-16)

❖

Conclusion

I want to conclude in this small BUT POWERFUL book on forgiveness with the fact that our individual and personal relationship with God is ABSOLUTELY EVERYTHING! I even want to suggest that it is only through our relationship with God, that we can overcome in any area of our lives, especially unforgiveness.

Our RELATIONSHIP with God should be the axis on which everything else in our life spins. He is the security under which we operate and without a personal relationship with God, we have a dead religion. Once we have received the revelation of His love for us and that we have been forgiven, it is much easier to express our love for God and forgiveness towards others. On the other hand, when we lose sight of what we have been forgiven of, we harden ourselves towards God and towards others.

> *This woman has been forgiven much, and she is showing much love. But the person who has shown little love shows how little forgiveness he has received.*
> *(Luke 7:47-48 VOICE)*

Our worship must centre on HIM, not on anything else and not just what we can GET out of Him. *"We love Him, because He first loved us"* (1 John 4:19). *Our relationship cannot just be about what we can accumulate.*

Our whole lives must be an expression of our love towards Him. Not just about how well we sing in church or how gifted we are in a specific area, but how well we treat others for example. Every motivation must be to bring Him glory. *"Whatever you do, do it all for the glory of God"* (1 Corinthians 10:31 NIV).

Lastly this scripture shows just how God holds us TOTALLY RESPONSIBLE to walk in forgiveness towards others.

> *[Now having received the Holy Spirit, and being led and directed by Him] if you forgive the sins of anyone, they are forgiven; if you retain the sins of anyone, they are retained.*
> *(John 20:23)*

❖

Prayer

*F*ather thank You for Your forgiveness in and through my life. Don't ever let me lose touch with the reality of Your forgiveness, so that I can walk in that same forgiveness towards others. Just as I have been forgiven, I want to freely forgive. I want to walk and live in a right spirit at all times. Help me daily in Jesus name. Amen.

Confession

I am governed by God's Spirit. I walk willingly in a Spirit of Forgiveness. I live at harmony with my brothers and sisters in the Body of Christ. I live at peace with those around me on a daily basis. My mouth is not a place of curse but blessing. My heart and my mouth belong to the Lord. I walk by the Spirit and His fruits define my behaviour today and every day of my life in Jesus' name.

❖

Helpful Scriptures

In Whom we have our redemption through His blood,
[which means] the forgiveness of our sins.

(Colossians 1:14)

In Him we have redemption (deliverance and salvation)
through His blood, the remission (forgiveness) of our
offenses (shortcomings and trespasses), in accordance
with the riches and the generosity of His gracious favor.

(Ephesians 1:7)

To open their eyes that they may turn from darkness to
light and from the power of Satan to God, so that they may
thus receive forgiveness and release from their sins and a

place and portion among those who are consecrated and purified by faith in Me.

(Acts 26:18)

So let it be clearly known and understood by you, brethren, that through this Man forgiveness and removal of sins is now proclaimed to you.

(Acts 13:38)

To Him all the prophets testify (bear witness) that everyone who believes in Him [who adheres to, trusts in, and relies on Him, giving himself up to Him] receives forgiveness of sins through His name.

(Acts 10:43)

God exalted Him to His right hand to be Prince and Leader and Saviour and Deliverer and Preserver, in order to grant repentance to Israel and to bestow forgiveness and release from sins.

(Acts 5:31)

And Peter answered them, Repent (change your views and purpose to accept the will of God in your inner selves instead of rejecting it) and be baptized, every one of you, in the name of Jesus Christ for the forgiveness of and release from your sins; and you shall receive the gift of the Holy Spirit.

(Acts 2:38)

And that repentance [with a view to and as the condition of] forgiveness of sins should be preached in His name to all nations, beginning from Jerusalem.

(Luke 24:47)

And everyone who makes a statement or speaks a word against the Son of Man, it will be forgiven him; but he who blasphemes against the Holy Spirit [that is, whoever intentionally comes short of the reverence due the Holy Spirit], it will not be forgiven him [for him there is no forgiveness].

(Luke 12:10)

To bring and give the knowledge of salvation to His people in the forgiveness and remission of their sins.

(Luke 1:77)

John the Baptist appeared in the wilderness (desert), preaching a baptism [obligating] repentance (a change of one's mind for the better, heartily amending one's ways, with abhorrence of his past sins) in order to obtain forgiveness of and release from sins.

(Mark 1:4)

For this is My blood of the new covenant, which [ratifies the agreement and] is being poured out for many for the forgiveness of sins.

(Matthew 26:28)

To the Lord our God belong mercy and loving- kindness and forgiveness, for we have rebelled against Him.

(Daniel 9:9)

❖

Bibliography

- Pateman, Dr. Alan. <u>Deliverance, A Present Reality</u>. Published by Merseyside Printing Co., Merseyside, UK, 1991.

- Prince, Derek. <u>Protection from Deception</u>. Published by Whitaker House, Springdale, Pennsylvania, USA, 2008.

- Robertson, Pat. <u>The Secret Kingdom</u>. Published by World Publishing, Dallas, Texas, USA, 1992.

- Robertson, Pat. <u>The Rewards of Repentance</u>. Published by 700 Club, CBN Europe Partner Report June 2013, Hereford, England UK, 2013.

- Strong's, James. <u>Exhaustive Concordance</u>. Touch Bible™ (KJV + Strong's Concordance), Copyright ©2011 Patrick Franklin.

- Unless otherwise indicated, Scripture quotations are taken from the Amplified® Bible, Copyright © 1954, 1958, 1962, 1964, 1965, 1987 by The Lockman Foundation. Used by permission. (www.Lockman.org)

- Scripture quotations marked ERV are taken from the Easy-to-Read-Version. Copyright © 2006 World Bible Translation Center.

❖

Ministry Profile

Doctor Alan Pateman, an apostle, is the President and Founder of **"Alan Pateman Ministries International"** (APMI), which was established in England back in 1987, a Christian-based *(parachurch)* non-profit and non-denominational outreach. This ministry is now focusing in two main areas: First **"Connecting for Excellence"** Apostolic Networking (CFE) and secondly, the teaching arm, **"LifeStyle International Christian University"** (LICU).

CFE is a multi-facetted missions organisation with the purpose of connecting leaders for divine opportunities and building lasting relationships, to touch the lives of leaders literally the world over. Apostle Dr Alan Pateman has to date ordained more than 500 ministers in over 50 NATIONS. In addition there are ministries, churches and schools who are in Association or Affiliation, looking to him for apostolic counsel and oversight.

Secondly LICU, which was founded in 2007, is a study program to help people discover their purpose and destiny. A global network of university campuses and correspondence students, demonstrating the Supernatural Kingdom of God through Doctrinal, Apostolic and Prophetic Teaching. Dr Alan holds the position of President/CEO, Professor of Theology, Biblical Studies and Apostolic Ministry. LICU is exploding throughout Europe, Asia and Africa, enhancing the Body of Christ

Dr Alan has authored more than 35 books including numerous teaching materials and LICU university courses (30) along with hundreds of Truth for the Journey articles on kingdom lifestyle *(that are regularly distributed globally via the internet).*

He is recognised as an Apostle, Bishop, Leadership Mentor, University Educator, Motivational Speaker, Connector and Author, who has also been featured on national and international TV and radio networks throughout the years.

Currently Apostle Alan, his wife Dr Jennifer reside in Lucca *(Tuscany)* Italy and travel out from their Apostolic Company.

- Alan Pateman Ph.D., D.Min., D.D., M.A., B.Th.

Academic Background

Dr. Alan Pateman attended several colleges throughout his training *(including studying Theology at Roffey Place, Horsham, UK and a Member of Kerygma - with Rev. Colin Urquhart and Dr. Bob Gordon - 1985-1987)* before being awarded a Doctorate of Divinity *(2006)* in recognition of his lifetime achievements by the International College of Excellence, now "DanEl Christian College" *(President: Dr. Robb Thompson USA)* also "Life Christian University" *(Dr. Douglas Wingate USA)* where he also earned a Bachelor of Theology B.Th. *(2006),* a Master of Arts in Theology M.A., a Doctor of Ministry in Theology D.Min., *(2007)* and Doctor of Philosophy in Theology Ph.D. *(2013)* from LICU.

❖

To Contact the Author

Please email:

Alan Pateman Ministries International

Email: apostledr@alanpateman.com
Web: www.AlanPatemanMinistries.com

*Please include your prayer requests
and comments when you write.*

❖

Other Books

Media, Spiritual Gateway

Let's face it; we live in the era of fake news! It's always existed, but never been quite so prominent. Today it's an all-out-war between fact and political fiction.

ISBN: 978-1-909132-54-2, Pages: 192,
Format: Paperback, Published: 2018
Also available in eBook format!

Millennial Myopia, From a Biblical Perspective

The standard for every generation is Jesus. However Millennial Myopia describes the trap of focusing everything on one particular generation or demographic cohort, at the exclusion and expense of all others. The Church cannot afford to make this mistake too.

ISBN: 978-1-909132-67-2, Pages: 216,
Format: Paperback, Published: 2017
Also available in eBook format!

Truth for the Journey Books

TONGUES, Our Supernatural Prayer Language

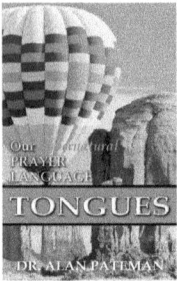

In writing to the church at Corinth, Paul encouraged them to continue the practice of speaking with other tongues in their worship of God and in their prayer lives as a means of spiritual edification. "He that speaketh in an unknown tongue edifies, charges, builds himself up like a battery."

ISBN: 978-1-909132-44-3, Pages: 144,
Format: Paperback, Published: 2016
Also available in eBook format!

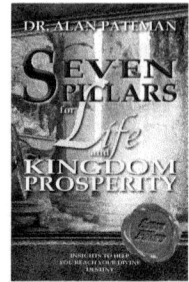

Seven Pillars for Life and Kingdom Prosperity

I submit these "Seven Pillars for Life and Kingdom Prosperity" to you, (Love, Prayer, Righteousness, Obedience, Connections, Management, Money). It's my desire that you walk in the triumphs that God has ordained for you.

ISBN: 978-1-909132-46-7, Pages: 220,
Format: Paperback, Published: 2016
Also available in eBook format!

Seduction & Control: Infiltrating Society & the Church

This book is a glance into the world of seduction and control, how they try to influence the Church through many powerful avenues such as the New Age, sexual education in our schools, basic entertainment; things that touch our everyday lives in order that we effectively and gradually become desensitised.

ISBN: 978-1-909132-00-9, Pages: 156
Format: Paperback, Published: 2015
Also available in eBook format!

Truth for the Journey Books

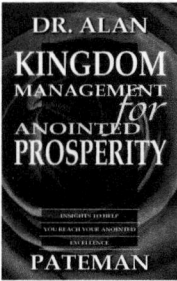

Kingdom Management for Anointed Prosperity

In his book, "Kingdom Management for Anointed Prosperity," Dr. Alan Pateman reveals how we can avoid living in continual crisis due to mismanagement. Life happens to all of us, but how we handle it matters most.

ISBN: 978-1-909132-34-4, Pages: 144, Format: Paperback, Published: 2015
Also available in eBook format!

Why War: A Biblical Approach to the Armour of God and Spiritual Warfare

Spiritual warfare means different things to different people, but from a biblical standpoint Ephesians 6:10-18 gives us the best biblical definition of spiritual warfare possible. We can also see how God has thoroughly equipped us for victory not just self defence!

ISBN: 978-1-909132-39-9, Pages: 180, Format: Paperback, Published: 2013
Also available in eBook format!

WINNING by Mastering your Mind

Someone once said, "Happiness begins between your ears and your mind is the drawing room for tomorrow's circumstances..." Remember, what happens in your mind will happen in time, and therefore one of our first priorities must be mind-management.

ISBN: 978-1-909132-40-5, Pages: 136, Format: Paperback, Published: 2017
Also available in eBook format!

Truth for the Journey Books

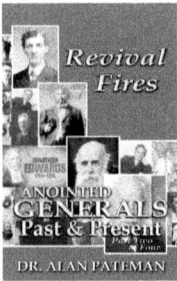

Revival Fires - Anointed Generals
Past & Present (Part Two of Four)

Seasons might be changing but God's Word remains the same. The heart of the author is to help train, equip and be a blessing to those men and women who will be willing to fulfil their potential in ministry and be properly equipped for service.

ISBN: 978-1-909132-36-8, Pages: 142,
Format: Paperback, Published: 2012
Also available in eBook format!

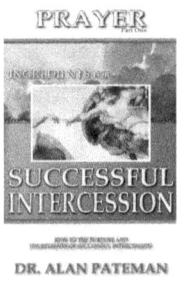

Prayer, Touching the Heart of God (Part Two)

Touching the Heart of God is the very essence of prayer. Whether we are petitioning God with very specific requests or consecrating ourselves before Him and rededicating our lives - whatever the case may be – the true essence of all praying is "Touching the Heart of God."

ISBN: 978-1-909132-12-2, Pages: 180,
Format: Paperback, Published: 2012
Also available in eBook format!

Prayer, Ingredients for Successful Intercession
(Part One)

This Book is the first of two books on Prayer. Dr. Pateman provides an exhaustive study, showcasing the vital ingredients necessary for all successful prayer. An excellent power-packed teaching tool, either for the individual or for the local church prayer group, that's eager to lay a solid foundation but don't know where to start!

ISBN: 978-1-909132-11-5, Pages: 140,
Format: Paperback, Published: 2012
Also available in eBook format!

Truth for the Journey Books

Apostles: Can the Church Survive Without Them?

Before Jesus returns a significant increase of the anointing will be poured out on the Body of Christ, but can the Church handle such an anointing? *(Acts 5:5)* Billy Brim once said, "As much as the anointing is powerful to create, it is as powerfully destructive of evil." The fear of God will be restored with the apostolic and people will begin walking with such anointing, as we have never seen before!

ISBN: 978-1-909132-04-7, Pages: 164, Format: Paperback, Published: 2012
Also available in eBook format!

Sexual Madness: In a Sexually Confused World

This book discusses the sensitive subject of political correctness in our world today and the growing fear of causing offence in the public arena. It also discusses the rise of homosexuality, pedophilia and all other forms of sexuality, as there are many. Including modern statistics on pornography.

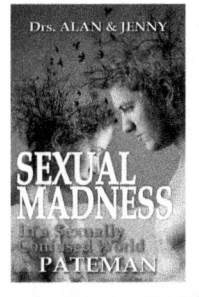

ISBN: 978-1-909132-02-3, Pages: 160, Format: Paperback, Published: 2012
Also available in eBook format!

His Life is in the Blood

Blood is the trophy of every battle. The spilt blood of Jesus Christ is our trophy. It is our freedom from sin and bondage. Nothing can enter the blood-bought temples of the Holy Ghost! This book will encourage you to apply the blood of Jesus our Passover Lamb to your life, just as the children of Israel did in the Old Testament. Not merely talking or reading about it, but applying it.

ISBN: 978-1-909132-06-1, Pages: 152, Format: Paperback, First Published: 2007
Also available in eBook format!

Dear Friends,

Have you considered becoming one of our international students? We are privileged to welcome you, from around the world, to "LifeStyle International Christian University" *(the teaching arm of Alan Pateman Ministries International).* **An English speaking university** dedicated to your success; to see you trained and equipped to fully succeed in your God given Destiny.

It is our passion to raise up the leaders of tomorrow, who will have influence in all realms of authority, including the Body of Christ. Men and women of strategy, wisdom and true godliness, who'll stand with stature and maturity in this hour.

It's undeniable that in today's world, recognised education has become indispensable, therefore it is our desire to offer well balanced and well structured courses. Those that have been written by gifted and talented ministers of God, who seek to be inspired by God's Holy Spirit.

Consequently we have put together a **flexible curriculum,** designed both for correspondence students and campuses, which is a strategy to reach the distant learner; whether provincial, national or international. In fact we have many correspondence students from around the world, including a growing number of successful campuses, in various countries.

This is a growing platform, where men and women of dignity and passion, can grow and be established in their God given endeavours. As God is the healer of the nations, we pray and believe that many of our alumni will go on to **become world changers** in their own right.

We are proud of each and every one of our LICU students.
It would be our pleasure if you would join them on this incredible journey!

Doctor Alan Pateman

Alan Pateman Prof. Ph.D., D.Min., D.D., M.A., B.Th.
PRESIDENT AND CEO
www.licuuniversity.com www.cfeapostolicnetwork.com
Email: info@licuuniversity.com Mob: +39 366 329 1315

For more information visit our website/facebook or contact our office, using the details below:

Website: www.licuuniversity.com
Facebook: www.facebook.com/LICUMainCampus
Email: info@licuuniversity.com
Telephone: +39 366 329 1315

Alan Pateman Ministries
Presents

Conference

CONNECTING FOR EXCELLENCE
Lucca Italy

An international apostolic
and prophetic network

YOUR HOSTS: ALAN PATEMAN   JENNIFER PATEMAN

apostledr@alanpateman.com, Tel. 0039 366 329 1315

W W W . A L A N P A T E M A N M I N I S T R I E S . C O M

Please contact our office or download the registration form.
Registration fee: €40

Partner with us TODAY!

We are looking to impact the world with the gospel, together we can do more! Join with us to equip the Body of Christ through our Apostolic Network, LICU university program, campuses, associated schools, missions, conferences, television programs, publication of articles and Truth for the Journey books.

You can become an APMI FOUNDATION PARTNER with a regular contribution of any amount, whether it is once a month or once a year.

- Receive monthly newsletters
- Connect with partners and leaders at our Connecting for Excellence international meetings
- Partners Dinners
- Personal availability for mentoring by Doctor Alan
- Enjoy complimentary books by Doctors Alan and Jennifer
- For those who GIVE EVERY MONTH £10, £15, £20, £30 or more will save money with special discounts on products, hotel rooms, conferences, and more

Partner With Us Today!
Call Italy: +39 366 3291315
Email: partners@alanpatemanministries.com
www.AlanPatemanMinistries.com

All Books Available

at

APMI PUBLICATIONS

Email: publications@alanpateman.com
*Also Available from Amazon.com
and other retail outlets.*

*If you purchased this book through Amazon.com
or other and enjoyed reading it, or perhaps one of
my other books, I would be grateful if you could
take a couple of minutes to write a Customer
Review, many thanks.*

www.ingramcontent.com/pod-product-compliance
Lightning Source LLC
Chambersburg PA
CBHW071601040426
42452CB00008B/1248